WOLVES

CONTENTS

Who's Afraid of the Big, Bad Wolf?	2-3
Face to Face	4-5
Wolf Worlds	6-9
It's a Tough Life	10-13
Pups and Packs	14-17
Communication	18-19
Wolf Relatives	20-23
Index	24

Who's Afraid of the Big, Bad Wolf

When I was a little boy, *Little Red Riding Hood* was one of my favorite stories. Wolf stories always gave me the shivers, but they fascinated me, too.

The first time I met wolves in the wild, their howls sent chills down my spine. But now a wolf howl thrills me, and I know that their amber eyes are curious, not cruel. My childhood fears of the Big, Bad Wolf have faded as I have learned more about wolves.

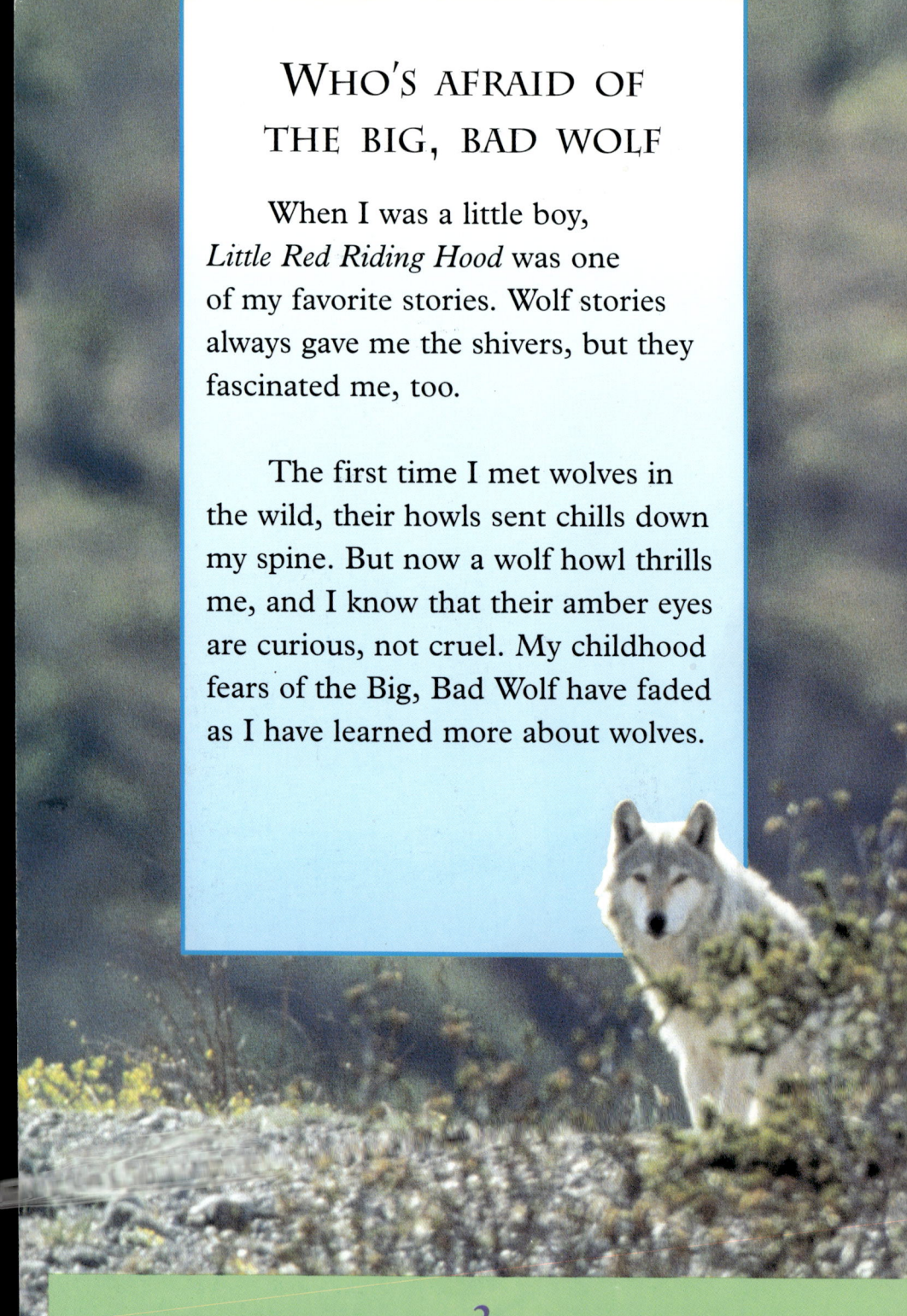

FACE TO FACE

My first meeting with a wolf came many years ago. I was photographing a young deer when suddenly it ran off. I turned to see a snarling wolf lying in front of its den! It let out a deafening howl – a signal to the other wolves to return.

I panicked and ran the wrong way. I could hear the howls of the other wolves as they got closer. It was growing dark, so I curled up in the hollow of a burned-out tree. A great horned owl hooted over my head.

I dozed for a while, then woke to see seven wolves sitting no more than twenty feet in front of me! They stared at me with their amber eyes. Then, they turned and trotted away. As soon as it was light, I made my way back to my cabin.

COYOTE

WOLF

Wolf worlds

I usually track and photograph gray wolves. There are two main types of gray wolf – the tundra wolf and the timber wolf. They can vary in color from black to white, although they're all called "gray wolves."

The timber wolf lives in the woods in subarctic regions. Black timber wolves are my favorite wolves to photograph. They can't be confused with large coyotes because of their distinctive color.

Timber wolves usually hunt moose, elk, bighorn sheep, or deer, depending on the local habitat. These local habitats vary from alpine mountains, where there are no trees, to thick pine forests.

Tundra wolves live inside the Arctic Circle. They are also called arctic wolves or white wolves. They are larger than timber wolves. Their size and thick winter coats help them survive the nine cold months of the arctic winter. Arctic wolves survive by hunting the large herds of caribou that roam across the frozen tundra.

At one time, wolves roamed all over the Northern Hemisphere. But wherever large numbers of people settled, they destroyed the wolves. Today, most wolves live in remote places in Canada, China, and Russia, and in Alaska, Minnesota, and Montana in the United States of America.

It's a tough life

Wild wolves have a tough life. It is sometimes hard to find enough food. Wolves rely on their excellent hearing and sense of smell to locate their prey. Their ability to see prey that isn't moving is poor. Perhaps that is why a deer stops when it hears a strange sound. All animals have a well-developed sense of survival. I have watched a mountain goat choose a cliff path too narrow for a hungry wolf pack to follow.

Sometimes the wolves will travel over a hundred miles to get enough food for the pack. In one study, it was found that a wolf pack might chase over a dozen moose before capturing one. That takes a lot of energy!

A wolf can run fast for a short distance, but a moose can run even faster. A moose can injure or kill a wolf with its hooves and antlers. A young wolf who attacks a porcupine may die from infection when the porcupine quills stick into its flesh.

Many wild wolves die from disease or injury, but man is their worst enemy. Wolves have always been hunted. Many have died from traps, poisoning, and gunshot wounds. Some hunters think that wolves wipe out game like elk and deer, and ranchers fear for their livestock.

PUPS AND PACKS

Wolf families live and hunt together in groups called packs. A pack usually has about six to ten wolves in it. A wolf pack's territory can extend as far as twenty miles from the den site. Every wolf pack marks its territory by urinating around the borders. The wolves also howl to make their territory known to others.

Every wolf knows its place in the pack. The two lead parents are called the *alpha male* and *alpha female*. The alpha male is easy to spot. He is always the leader as they walk in single file.

The next leaders of the pack are called the *beta male* and *beta female*. The beta male will become the leader when the alpha male is too old to lead, or is injured or killed. The beta female watches the wolf pups and cares for them throughout their early life.

The alpha female chooses a safe denning site in the early spring. The pups are born in the last weeks of spring. At birth, wolf pups weigh about one pound. They are blind, deaf, and helpless. At first they live only on mother's milk, but after about three weeks, they begin to eat meat. The other mature wolves help to raise the pups by hunting for their food and protecting them in the den.

The playful pups grow quickly over the summer and receive a lot of attention from the adult pack members. The pack abandons the den when the pups are about two months old. They move to an unsheltered area called a rendezvous site. By autumn, the pups and adults begin to hunt together as a pack.

17

COMMUNICATION

If a member doesn't like its rank in the wolf pack, it can challenge the leaders or leave the territory and become a lone wolf. This behavior helps keep the pack from becoming too large. Sometimes a lone male and female will answer one another's howls and join up to start a new wolf family in a territory of their own.

Communication is an important part of wolf life. This is done by howling, barking, and growling, and through gestures such as lowering the head or tucking the tail between the legs. Howling is very important and allows the pack to join up after becoming separated during a hunt. It also warns neighboring packs to stay out of the pack's territory.

WOLF RELATIVES

Dogs are descendants of wolves. Wild wolves were probably attracted to early human settlements by the smell of meat. People took wolf pups from dens and raised them. Eventually people and the wolf dogs became friends. People provided food and shelter.

The dogs guarded camp. Large dogs could carry heavy loads. Small dogs made excellent guard dogs. They always barked when a stranger approached. Early dogs also pulled sleds when people moved their settlements to follow and hunt migrating herds of bison or caribou.

People also domesticated other wild animals such as sheep and oxen to make their lives easier. Later, dogs helped by herding flocks of sheep and guarding over them.

Most dogs don't look like their wolf ancestors, but some things have stayed the same. All dogs give birth to pups sixty-three days after breeding – just like the wild wolf.

Wolf and dog behavior is also very similar. Both bark and growl when angry or frightened. Some dogs like to howl like a wild wolf. And both dogs and wolves wag their tails when they are happy. Perhaps you have noticed your dog follows its tail in a circle before lying down. I have seen wild wolves do the same thing.

Dogs are called "man's best friend." I hope that man can become the wolves' best friend and make sure that they always have places where they can roam freely.

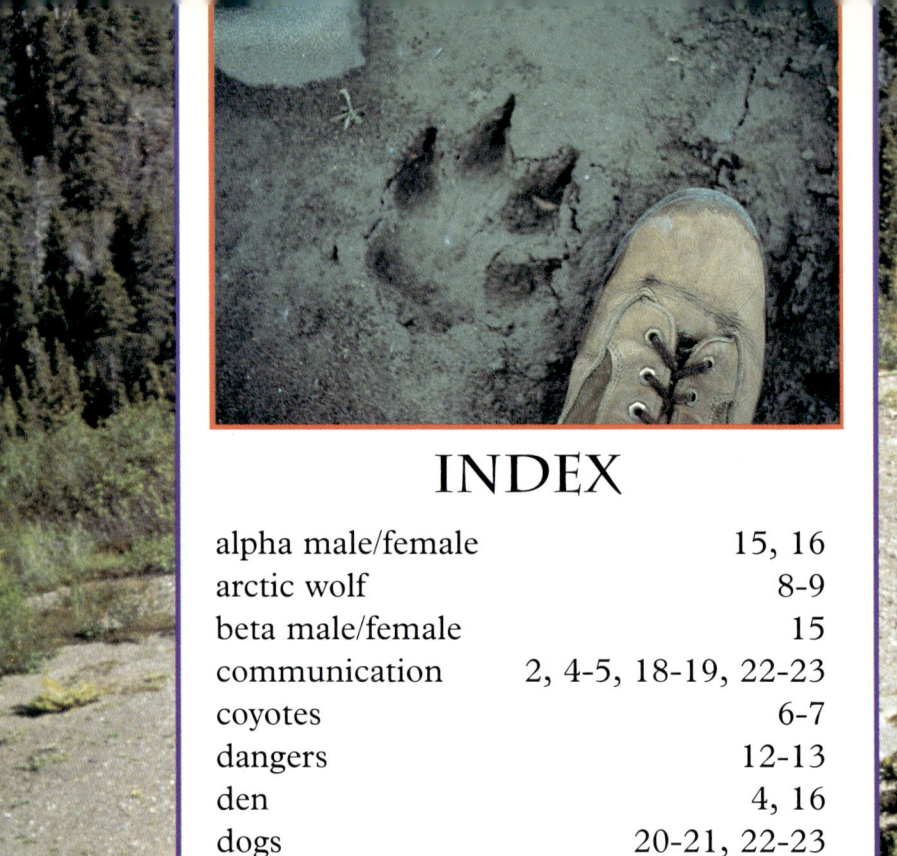

INDEX

alpha male/female	15, 16
arctic wolf	8-9
beta male/female	15
communication	2, 4-5, 18-19, 22-23
coyotes	6-7
dangers	12-13
den	4, 16
dogs	20-21, 22-23
geographical regions	7, 9
gray wolf	6-7
habitat	7
hunting	9, 10-11, 16
Little Red Riding Hood	2
lone wolf	18
packs	10, 15, 16, 18-19
prey	7, 8-9, 10-11
pups	15, 16-17, 22
rank	18
territory	14-15
timber wolf	7
tundra wolf	7, 8-9